"In Conversations with Strangers, Marg Gibbs creates a shimmering patina for life. Through her blog-style entries, she speaks of the enrichment gained from her creativity and sharing moments with strangers. And she encourages us to wear our skin lightly, so that we too might experience life more fully and joyfully, aware of the simple, important things."
– Janeen Brian, award-winning author

"Conversations with Strangers contains a well-balanced mix of thoughtful reflection and helpful advice. Sensitive and heartfelt, it will guide you towards living a life of joy and connection with others. The inspirational quotes and poems are a delightful bonus."
– Aleesah Darlison, award-winning author, presenter, guest speaker and owner of Greenleaf Agency

"This bricolage of memories and observations of life is very personal, but is also motivational to readers. With simple words, Marg paints pictures of the joy of becoming aware of – and connecting with – nature, people and the inhabited world. Her ability to notice and note provides a gentle direction for all who seek to enrich their lives."
– Sorrel Edwards

Dedicated to my family, Andrew, Lachlan, Tim and Rachael – the four treasures in my life.

And to Bill Smith, my soul mate: one I consider no stranger at all.

Conversations with Strangers

The art of creativity and connection

by
M J Gibbs

Conversations with Strangers
M J Gibbs

© Marg Gibbs 2020

www.mjgibbs.com.au
m.j.gibbs@bigpond.com

While this book is intended as a general information resource and all care has been taken in compiling the contents, this book does not take account of individual circumstances and is not in any way a substitute for professional advice. Always consult with a qualified practitioner or therapist. Neither the author nor the publisher and their distributors can be responsible for any loss, claim or action that may rise from reliance on the information contained in this book.

All rights reserved. This book may not be reproduced in whole or part, stored, posted on the internet, or transmitted in any form or by any means, electronic, mechanical, photocopying, recording, or other, without permission from the author of this book.

Editing, design and publishing support by www.AuthorSupportServices.com

ISBN: 978-0-6486638-1-2

A catalogue record for this book is available from the National Library of Australia

Table of Contents

Introduction 1

Travel 5

Nature 21

Loneliness 35

Celebration 49

Seasons 61

Quietude 75

Empathy 85

Food 97

Love 109

Art 121

Writing 131

Goals 143

Final musings 155

Acknowledgements 160

Want to continue the conversation? 161

Introduction

Why Conversations with Strangers?

It was a phrase that my daughter wrote on a birthday card that inspired this book.

She said I was a "seasoned conversationalist with perfect strangers."

That's me. How true.

A few facts about me: the Chinese horoscope tells me I'm a Rooster. My four adult children call me 'Goose', a sweet nickname. I also answer to Grandma and my husband calls me his chick!

Beyond this, I love children's books, art and travelling. For the best part of 25 years, I've immersed myself in secondary English teaching, along with history and social sciences. Not surprisingly, with this background, I set demanding goals for myself that involve creativity and connection.

Growing up in Brisbane with a brother, a sister, a father who debated Christianity and a mother who regularly attended church, my bicycle and I were best friends. Riding my bike not only took me places but also brought me freedom and connection to others. I had many cousins and good friends at school, but I was happy in my own company too.

Perhaps that's because I've always been a creative person? I know I enjoy using my hands to make things and experiment. And now that I'm all grown up and retired from teaching, you'll often find me going up to complete strangers and connecting with them in spontaneous ways.

In the light of my daughter's comment, I can't help reflecting that this is another example of my creative approach. In the end, I decide to write about it.

I am interested in the way people talk

I'm fascinated by people's stories and their conversations. Speaking to strangers is often an eye-opening experience for me that can spark meaningful interaction and connection. Those fleeting moments in an elevator, bus station or supermarket can help me fall in love with the world or give me a glimpse into another's lifestyle. It's a reciprocal exchange.

And yet, to some people, it can feel like they're invisible and unwelcome.

I very rarely plan to find strangers to talk to. Noticing other people and reaching out to connect with them simply works its magic in me as part of my creative personality.

So, on the surface, this book is about the ways in which I start conversations with others to extend connection. It's about opening myself up to another person's mind, thoughts and feelings.

In that way, *Conversations with Strangers* is a book that's both personal and universal in its approach.

Speaking with strangers brings a unique kind of joy

Whenever I have a sustained conversation with someone I don't know, I find a surprising thread of happiness running through it. Perhaps one person brings me new insight and revelation. Or there may be a pleasant energy between me and the other person that quietly touches me.

It's been so enriching for me to broaden my views of life and gain new perspectives through these conversations. Plus, it's often easier to unload my stories onto strangers. Could it perhaps be because I might never see them again? I know little about them, so perhaps in sharing my heart and connecting to their story, I uncover more truth about myself.

Regardless, I'm sure you understand the desire to escape from the same-sameness of 'normal life' and daily routines. The good news is that you can. All it takes is to let yourself experience the unexpected surprises that come when you reach out and connect to another person you don't know.

When you do this, I think you'll be delighted by the revelations of new perspectives and fresh ideas – and, most of all, at the spontaneous joy they spark.

In this book, I'm hoping to share that joy with you

As you read through the 12 chapters of *Conversations with Strangers*, you'll encounter the 12 themes that have most inspired me and that continue to give me strength. You'll see how the concepts of family, love, creativity and connection are each interwoven with, and reflected in, the chance conversations I've had with strangers.

Sprinkled through each chapter, you'll find personal stories, poems, inspirational quotes and questions to ask yourself. There are photographs I've taken that simply and directly illustrate the concepts of connection and creativity. And at the end of each chapter, there are activities to help you build on the theme we've explored together. I encourage you to complete one, two or all of these activities from the chapter you've just read before you go on to the next one.

However your journey through these pages looks, though, I hope you can learn to observe, be aware of and consider other people you don't currently know. I hope you think about how you might open up more to joy and spontaneity in your life.

Whether your conversation ends up being a polite encounter, free advice, a question or a deeper reflection, speaking to someone you don't know can take you on a happy journey.
And who knows? By the time you get to the end, maybe you'll be ready to go out and strike up your own conversations with strangers.

Cheers,

Marg Gibbs

Conversations with Strangers

Travel

> " I came to your shore as a stranger , I lived in your house as a guest, I leave your door as a friend, my earth.
>
> – Rabindranath Tagore

Travelling develops my creativity

Do you like to travel? Tramp, wander, venture forth or dillydally? Seek adventure or mystery?

Do you enjoy seeing new places?

I like to think that travelling makes one creative.

I know that, for me, it provides endless opportunities to observe, reflect and embrace new ideas. It's an exposure to so many different ways of doing things. It lets me see things in different ways, including fresh solutions to problems and new interpretations.

For example, travelling broadens one's cultural, artistic endeavours by allowing one to step into new worlds. The worlds of music, landscapes and people. The worlds of wealth and poverty, of plain and ornate, of sweet and sour. It opens up worlds of cultural diversity.

To be creative, I buy myself a new diary and keep all my scribbled notes in a folder labelled 'OVERSEAS HOLIDAY'.

TRAVEL

My trip starts as soon as I begin to plan...

When I'm travelling overseas, I print off a weekly calendar from the internet with space to write down some notes. Because I'm a visual person, I use highlighters, symbols like stars or asterisks, and sticky notes to alert me to an action plan.

If this sounds too complicated or organised, it really isn't. It's just the way I do things.

I do this before I travel to southern France and northern Italy with Bill, my then-fiancé. We're experimenting and keen to explore, so we choose southern France as our destination.

I'm a slow planner, yet it's part of the joyful journey – to savour reading travel blogs, testimonies and reviews to expand my global knowledge. It's also a genuine way of connecting to others who've travelled to similar places, so I can understand their perspectives and travel tips.

Dive right in, no dillydallying or dawdling. Pen to paper. A plan.

The journey begins.

TRAVEL

Soon, we're in Europe

We start in Provence, where a stranger helps us out

Fast forward a few months and presto, Bill and I are in the beautiful provincial village of Bonnieux in southern France.

I find the perfect stranger to talk to – a woman who speaks little English, yet she helps us find our accommodation. This friendly, small woman offers to get into her car so we can follow her to the right address because we're lost. Quietly, we communicate easily with a nod, gesture and smile.

I'm grateful for her help and kindness. This connection brings a calm that means, after we arrive and unpack, I can enjoy a relaxed afternoon with Bill. Together, we watch the sun set on the most perfect French setting. The fragrant smell of earth and vineyard complements a perfect artist's canvas. It's a piece of paradise. Did we really leave Australia behind?

As I write in my journal, the world looks spectacular. In this serene place, creativity comes to me from the beautiful landscape and palette of colours. The light is subtle, creating the softness of spring.

As Lao Tzu said, "Nature does not hurry, yet everything is accomplished."

The days are full of new encounters, with anticipation that follows me around like a purring cat.

TRAVEL

Then, we move on to Nîmes, where a cyclist takes our photo

In Nîmes, Bill and I wander the boulevards and lined cobblestone paths to take in the splendour of this town. We wander and watch. We dillydally on the cobblestones, away from the tourists.

A fit cyclist stops us at the bridge to ask whether we want a photograph. Naturally, the conversationalist in me says, "YES!"

He tells us that he has a day off work and rides 100km from Montpellier and back to enjoy these moments. Impressed with his stamina and determination, we talk to him about Australia, travel and teaching.

This perfect stranger enlightens the day with his French personality, smile and charm. This connection then filters through the rest of the day. I like to think that we are the lucky ones who can open our hearts and minds to talk to someone we don't know. We pause, listen and catch a glimpse of a new insight.

The Frenchman rides away to another destination.

The local markets are fabulous to visit and connect us with others. We see ceramics, linens, handbags and souvenirs. Ripe cherries and apricots, crisp apples and strawberries are all laid out in rowed baskets. The colour red captures my attention. Vibrant RED, spicy and seductive. Red high heels. Red lipstick. Red dress. Red tablecloth.

It's a colour that shouts out at you with its Ferrari vibrancy.

TRAVEL

Finally, we leave France for Venice – city of canals and masks

Travelling to Italy allows us to immerse ourselves in watery scenes of boats with striped gondoliers pushing their oars through the canals. There are masks and more masks.

Even when we get lost and sidetracked in the mazes of Venice, creative ideas and strangers mingle where we least expect them. We see them side by side, on a bridge, at St Mark's Square or in a café.

I remember back to Paris when we saw African masks behind the glass windows. Intense, eerie eyes gazed out at me, impersonal and warrior-like. I wondered about them then. I wondered about how people hid behind personas that covered up their feelings and emotions. Those personas were masks that controlled the wearer and their actions, masks that overshadowed their inner world. They reminded me of a happy smile outside that covered a deep sadness within.

As humans, we share so many similar emotions of fear, grief, happiness and loneliness. And often, our masks change.

Now, in Venice, I'm reminded of the Chinese 'changing faces' operas, where performances on stage dazzle audiences. How is it possible to change from a red mask to a black in the twinkling of an eye? From a scowl to a smile? From a feeling of gratitude to regret? From vulnerability to ugliness?

I conclude that just because I'm selective about what I reveal to the world, it doesn't mean I'm insincere. Phoniness only happens when we lie about what's really going on inside.

TRAVEL

There's so much opportunity for creativity and connection

Travelling can be a strong motivator to be creative and connect to others. Creative ideas are sparked on trains, planes or buses, or at sea.

In the bustling crowds, in a piazza, museum, market or side street, I see the homeless, the wealthy and the laid-back tourists going about their day. I watch the striding gentleman wearing his stylish hat, the girl running in torn jeans and the toddler bending with the panda overalls. I turn just slightly and see the old man hobbling with his walking stick, the Irish busker playing his guitar and the backpacker stooping with his heavy load.

When I stop and watch for a moment, I see amazing possibilities in the snippets of life. Creativity is the ability to perceive the world in new ways, to find hidden patterns and to make connections between seemingly unrelated things.

Bill and I have had conversations with Italian waiters in Venice and Lake Como, chatted to a mother from Canada in Paris, bumped into Californians in Aix-en-Provence twice in one day and eaten a Guinness pie in Dublin. The memories that each conversation created add sparkle and fun to our lives.

I don't feel threatened by the unfamiliar faces of others from different cultures. I like to think that's who I am – a seasoned conversationalist, specialising in strangers. Even when I may never see someone again, I take pride in the possibilities of connecting with them.

Little things going wrong sometimes even lead you to a perfectly enjoyable conversation later on.

After all, troubles in a day make for interesting conversation.

TRAVEL

Questions to ask yourself

- Where would you like to travel to? What if you went out of your comfort zone?
- Is there a faraway place that beckons you?
- Are you shy or willing to take risks?
- How can you record new ideas when travelling?
- Can you start up a new conversation without feeling anxious?

Activities to Try

- ✓ Plan a new travel route.
- ✓ Buy a new atlas.
- ✓ Create a checklist for overseas travels.
- ✓ Keep a gratitude travel diary.
- ✓ Use a pink highlighter on a map to show where you've been.

nature

> " Look deep into nature, and then you will understand everything better.
> – Albert Einstein

Nature is full of surprises

Not quite winter in Mapleton, June brings chill and anticipation.

I love that this month is a girl's name. I also love that June surprises me with beautiful growth in the garden. Geraniums, lavender, the lush growth of herbs like rosemary and thyme, gardenias that bloom and the natives that entice the birds. Honey scents and jasmine blooms.

Nature itself paints a canvas of new ideas.

As Ralph Waldo Emerson said, "Earth laughs in flowers."

NATURE

23

I'm blessed with an abundance of nature around me

Bill and I live in Mapleton – a picturesque village on the northern end of the scenic Blackall Range in the Sunshine Coast Hinterland.

Travel two hours north of Brisbane and you'll find the Blackall Ranges. Here, it is bliss. This is our home, where the black cockatoos gather in the branches to watch us and the air up on the mountains is a little cooler.

Mapleton has a beautiful, tranquil setting with a view across the valley to the ocean. The picturesque towns of Kureelpa and Dulong are dotted in the distance, with Mount Coolum visible and the Maroochy river a little further off creating a greener place.

This is our natural landscape.

We have a plethora of nature walks around us too. Close by are the Mapleton Falls lookout, The Great Walks and Kondalilla National Park. The Blackall Ranges is a landscape created by volcanoes and sculpted by water over millions of years, and it's only half an hour's drive from the Sunshine Coast.

It's a wondrous, invigorating place.

NATURE

Being in nature also helps me to connect

I've noticed how transformative nature is to my mind and body.

Bill and I often turn to nature for reward and inspiration. Today, we decide to walk along The Great Walks towards Ubajee.

Bill and I amble along the bush track. The morning is sunny with rainforest around us. Bird calls echo through the trees and the scent of eucalypts drifts in the air, when a woman and her dog come along.

At first, I notice how fit she looks and that – apart from her furry companion – she's by herself.

We greet each other with a smile and I ask her how often she walks here. She replies, "Often." Apparently, this is her daily escape and exercise regime.

She has a Scottish accent, so I ask her where in Scotland she grew up. I'm stunned when she replies, "Falkirk." That's the area between Edinburgh and Glasgow where my father grew up: Avonbridge village in Falkirk.

Immediately, I'm curious.

This perfect stranger tells us she is a doctor who discovered her husband while water skiing in Australia. Her furry friend is Bonnie – a fine Scottish name. She tells me her name is Audrey and I'm struck by the coincidence, because I have a granddaughter called Audrey.

She tells me too that both she and her husband enjoy the outdoors and that he's a good skier. It's a short, pleasant conversation in a peaceful place of beauty.

Our walk offers us more than just conversations

Bill and I continue on our way. Afterwards, I feel elated, surprised and joyful to have spoken to this intelligent woman.

Our friendly conversation taught me to pause and engage, to listen and learn. I liked that she was bold, regularly finding her own time to walk in the morning.

Bill and I both like the feelings of calm and rejuvenation that nature offers us. It's well known that walking boosts creativity too. Take it from bestselling author J K Rowling, who said, "Nothing like a night time stroll to give you ideas." Evidently, it works for her!

Later, along the Obi Obi Road in Mapleton, I encounter a few like-minded people who are out for their morning exercise as well. Usually, I offer a "Good morning!" or a simple "Hey." If they have a canine companion with them, I ask, "How's the dog?" Or I can always talk about the weather.

Paying attention is part of meeting others when you're hiking on a track.

There's a connection in noticing, for example, that someone is wearing an image of Yosemite National Park – or the Great Wall of China or Alaskan wildlife – on the front of a t-shirt. The connection brings a smile and an opening to ask the wearer, "How was your holiday?" This can be a starting point for a broader conversation, a small door I can open to connect more deeply with others.

The beauty of nature in itself is stunning

Bill and I love to observe and listen in the outdoors. It helps if we sit in a park, walk along a bush track or eat in the garden with friends. Nature always brings us new sounds and smells: the rain, the earth and the wind. Sometimes, our inner voices come to life in more gentle ways.

Leaves fall. Clouds shift. Birds sing. These are little treasures that drop onto your lap.

Another beautiful aspect of connecting with nature is feeling refreshed and less anxious. If you're usually hesitant to talk to others, take comfort in nature's ability to almost magically melt away that hesitance.

I remember a friend Shannyn saying when talking about going to bed: "... with the sinking of the sun, feeling the warmth drain out of the earth, and rising with the trill of the birds and the breaking of the day." She talked about how powerfully seductive that feeling was in its simplicity.

I muse that a large part of the seduction is nature's transformative power to clear one's head.

In nature, there are escarpments, hills, waterfalls and wildlife, all combining into a canvas of textures and sensory delights. The layers of beauty and surprise – diversity and reflection – await me around every corner and pathway.

I experience this at Mary Cairncross Scenic Reserve, impressed by its 55 hectares of National Estate listed subtropical rainforest. I pay attention, noticing the small details – the new bud, the golden leaf, the torn bark on trees, the clicking sound of cicadas in the evenings, the blustery winds and the scents of eucalypts.

But you don't need to travel far to experience that sense. There's nothing better than spending time in the garden, a nearby park or the bush. Just close your eyes, feel the warm breeze on your skin and let your mind wander.

Questions to ask yourself

- ✎ Do you make time to appreciate nature?
- ✎ Are you grateful for nature's grandeur?
- ✎ Can you journal about the natural beauty around you?
- ✎ Does your heart sing when you're close to nature?
- ✎ At night, do you pay attention to the moon?

Activities to try

- ✓ Walk with a child in a bush setting.
- ✓ Listen to nature music.
- ✓ Write a poem about the beauty of nature.
- ✓ Research Shinrin-Yoku (forest bathing).
- ✓ Camp under the stars and sleep with the smell of the earth.

Extra reflection

My friend and teaching colleague Shannyn remembers a time she went camping atop Brinkley Bluff in the West Macdonald Ranges. She tells me:

After five days of walking, my hiking buddy and I watched the sun set over a magnificent and vast landscape. We woke early to watch it rise again to warm the earth after a cold and windy night.

That experience, that opportunity to witness dusk and dawn in the same place, in the middle of my country, will stay with me forever. The magnitude of it is a highlight in my life, and the stunning awesomeness of it still delights me when I think of it.

loneliness

> " Loneliness ... allows your soul room to grow.
> – Janet Fitch

LONELINESS

Loneliness can be a cold, heavy ache

Winter in Mapleton is a time of brisk, cold winds and crackling fires. The mist covers the mountain and valley like a ghostly blanket. The garden is bleak, wilting in places. Darkness comes early.

I slide my feet into my cosy, warm slippers and enjoy eating Bill's tasty, spicy casserole for dinner. The aroma of beef and red wine gravy is intoxicating. This creative act in the kitchen prepares me for an emotional response.

Loneliness sneaks in because there's a stuck-inside kind of feeling wrapped around me.

It shivers beside me when I feel a sense of distance from others.

I feel nostalgic for the past and grieve loved ones, past and present.

The solitude of winter reminds me to reach out and make phone calls to people who are important to me.

One way of maintaining intimacy is to make shared memories

To bring in some creativity, I write down the names of friends I want to reconnect with, adding a star next to those who are my top priority. Then I tick off each person's name as I connect with them.

It's an intentional act that helps me to live more in the moment. Having a sense of purpose related to friends or family members provides opportunities for me to care more deeply and to feel valued, alive and less lonely.

This simple act of writing down names brings my attention to caring and connection, reducing the loneliness ache that can hit me at times. It helps me to laugh unexpectedly and think in a different way.

It helps me to appreciate the simple things in life.

Sometimes, strangers offer more comfort and calm than loved ones

My parents' deaths make me feel lonely and sad. Both of them are out of reach now. One died slowly with cancer, the other fast with an aneurysm. I feel a loss of intimate connection. I feel like an orphan.

I need an empathetic friend, one who understands this loss.

Comforting words written on cards lessen the hurt a little. But the truth is that I can no longer hear my father's voice, smell his cigarette smoke or discuss my Christian faith with him. I can't listen to my mother's mutterings, smell her powdery, soft hands or repeat things that she needs to hear me say. I can't throw my arms around either of them and give them a daughter's kiss anymore.

My hurt is different from my brother's or sister's, but that's okay.

Still, I notice small things triggering my tears. Seeing tartan fabric and listening to bagpipes play on Anzac Day tightens my throat. Hearing a sermon in a Mother's Day church service makes my eyes well up.

During these times, I hope for empathy and understanding from others. I long for them to identify with my sorrow and loss, and offer their kindness and remembrance.

Eventually, the grief and loneliness pass

So often, when I least expect it, pain comes. Vulnerability surfaces. I notice my weariness, my wariness, my irritability and tension. I recognise the way I brace myself against life. The pain comes with pandemonium in my soul, piercing my emotions with its sting.

But five years roll on. Slowly, I gain solace and acceptance that my life is shaped by both of my parents' values and the love they gave to me. I recognise my connections to them and their connections to me and others. I come to terms with their generous giving and their sacrifice.

I accept that I was their first-born child, and it shaped my life in so many ways afterwards.

I recognise that it's all part of the cycle of life.

LONELINESS

Sometimes I still reach out for the comfort of strangers

Now that I've come to terms with the deaths of my parents and accepted their absence, I talk to complete strangers about my mourning process. I often discover that they understand my emptiness and loneliness in ways my own family aren't sensitive to.

Often, strangers offer a gentle approach in times when my family are too blunt and busy with the mundaneness of their everyday living. Or is it perhaps easier to unload my burdens of grief onto casual acquaintances, rather than bring the subject up with family members? I can tell a stranger that it's the anniversary of my mother's passing with no expectation that they'd recognise the importance of the day. It's perhaps harder to talk to my own family when they simply forget or don't want to discuss it.

And so, sometimes, that unknown person in the supermarket queue can lessen my pain and offer a temporary release.

LONELINESS

The cure for loneliness is connection

I feel the loneliness ache often: the inner pain that comes with the sense that one doesn't belong. It's not necessarily a feeling of sadness – just one of real emptiness. As Mother Teresa said, "Loneliness and the feeling of being unwanted is the most terrible poverty."

To help overcome loneliness, we need to create rituals, celebrations and memories that strengthen our bonds. We need to keep in touch with old friends and genuinely care about their lives. We need to search out and rekindle past connections.

And, sometimes, we need to connect with a stranger.

Many people use online apps like Instagram and Pinterest to connect. Facebook can reunite people in serendipitous ways.

Some people even take Uber rides to find connection.

In the offline world, school reunions have a way of gathering people from all backgrounds. And, sometimes, we fill the emptiness with charity work and volunteering.

Loneliness is sadness caused by distance, which makes me wonder if people need to make more effort to shift their perspective to bridge that distance.

How would we reconnect if we recognised that life is to be lived and valued?

It's a thought-provoking exercise that's worth considering.

Questions to ask yourself

- When do you feel the loneliest?
- What do you need most when you're lonely? Why?
- How can you overcome lonely times in your life?
- Can you sit and talk with someone who has strong emotions?

Activities to Try

- ✓ Make enquiries about joining a new group.
- ✓ Reach out to someone who's positive and responsible.
- ✓ Find a hobby that includes others.
- ✓ Give a gift to someone. Connect.
- ✓ Learn closeness and then model it for others.

Extra reflection

The Loneliest Cat

Slinking against the wall
purring in the night
waiting for
his owner
to come
Home.

Waiting.

Curled up
a rope of wet fur
out in the rain
shivering for
his owner
to come
Home.

Jingling a bell
dallying in the day
a windy, zippy,
glad-to-see
owner
comes
Home.

M J Gibbs

Sharing memories and grief with a stranger

Over my lifetime, I've lost three border collies that each were a part of my family and my life. The sadness of that loss brings an emptiness and adjustment that many strangers easily understand.

I mention it in passing to my regular pest control man as he's doing his annual spray. Sadly, he tells me that his little dog Ella is no longer with him. He feels lonely without her in the house and misses her riding on his surfboard at the beach.

A simple conversation connects us through shared grief.

celebration

❝ The more you praise and celebrate your life, the more there is in life to celebrate.

– Oprah Winfrey

Celebrations help us move beyond the everyday

Birthdays, significant milestones, celebrations – we all enjoy them. Whether it's a baby's first birthday or an eightieth celebration, there's a sense of gratitude that life has brought blessings.

Some celebrations – like the traditional Hogmanay (Scottish New Year) – welcome friends and strangers with warm hospitality and, of course, lots of kissing. Scots like my father celebrated the New Year with revelry and passion. In my mind, I can hear 'Auld Lang Syne' – probably Robert Burns's most famous poem – being played. I can see the fireworks and imagine the festivities.

Celebrations help us to connect with others.

They bring joy and creativity, shifting us away from the same-sameness of everyday routines.

My 60th birthday demands more than just a single celebration

Because I'm a list-maker, I plan two events to celebrate my sixtieth birthday. One is with my children and grandchildren in a lovely park. The other is a French-themed dinner party at home with close friends.

First, I party with my family in the park

On a crisp, bright day at Russell Park in Montville, my family (four children, their partners and ten grandchildren) arrive for my birthday celebration. I've brought hessian sacks for the grandchildren to race in, plus balloons, balls and plenty of energy.

We quickly spread out over a blanket on the grass and seats near a central picnic table. The table brims with food, cake and presents.

There's a winter chill in the air and the trees are losing their leaves. A few other children play on swings nearby. The cousins get along well, chasing the dogs in the park. One grandson has brought a noisy, battery-operated whirly gig that flies through the air.

Before long, a young father and toddler (both strangers) walk towards us. Without thinking, I invite them to share in some of our snacks.

The little girl sits on the rug and happily eats popcorn with one of my granddaughters. My daughter looks at me as if to say, "Who is this man?" and my sons chuckle to themselves. They offer a polite exchange of greeting.

This brief, unexpected happening adds a layer to the day, a bit like the icing on a cake.

It might not seem normal, but I see a moment of opportunity to welcome a stranger and I go with it.

The little girl and her father thank us for the hospitality and move on to the slippery slide.

CELEBRATION

Later, I share a more structured celebration with friends

From an outdoor party to an indoor, French-themed dinner, the creativity flows to deepen my social connections. Unlike my first encounter with the anonymous father and daughter who join us at the picnic, the guest list for my birthday dinner party is carefully planned. There are no surprises or twists. The conversations come from familiar, long-term friendships.

The recent trip to France with its memorabilia and photos seems like a good place to start planning. A friend from Brisbane helps me with cooking, serving and cleaning up. Organisation and more formal planning are the keys to this dinner – unlike the throw-together, picnic-style routine. Bill is a terrific help and support too, even though he struggles with larger group entertaining. I like the way he stands tall and listens, watches the guests and then makes himself known.

To plan out the French theme, I browse the internet, visit homeware shops, read decorator magazines and talk to friends. After all, my 60th is a special occasion and I'm motivated to spend time planning the evening in detail.

Inspired by our recent trip to Provence, I include a banner, an Eiffel Tower ornament, a 'Bon Appétit' sign, a few French postcards and some rosé wine.

I make lists. I write down guest names and start gathering supplies like a bowerbird. Then I design the invitations. Find tablecloths. Think about what to wear. I remember to pick the French lavender in our garden.

One idea leads to another until it seems my head is full of 'party planning'. Ideas can wake me during the night, and when they do, I take note of them.

Creativity is a bit like strangers – both can come unexpectedly, both are useful.

These are the creative ideas I use to plan my picnic and French dinner party:

Picnic in the park

- A poem
- A family portrait
- Canvas art with the grandchildren's hand-prints
- Dress ups
- Gift voucher for a massage
- Sack races
- Party bags
- Photo board
- Scavenger hunt
- Stilts
- Rugs
- Jugs of water
- Balloon bust game

Dinner party with French theme

- Black and white postcards made into bunting with string and pegs
- Menu boards
- French bookmark in wine glasses
- Berets and stripes
- Lemons and lavender on the table
- Café signs
- French words
- Bon Appétit sign
- French apron
- Provencal tablecloths / rosé wine
- Quiz games – French cuisine
- Movies
- Song and recital music

Celebrating opens the door to creativity

Celebrating special events (birthdays, weddings, baby showers or hen's parties) often leads to a flurry of creative ideas and intuitive emotion.

And after simple ideas for entertaining are put together, the occasion itself and the guests often bring another rich layer. I believe it's good to trust your guests and friends to add their own sparkle of wit and banter.

In such a mix, creative ideas flow. The possibilities are surprising.

For example, in your next celebration, think about how fabric – in all its richness of texture, colour and pattern – can complement any party theme. Perhaps try:

- ✓ festoons under the moon for outdoors
- ✓ bohemian and mismatched patterns in your canopy for a relaxed picnic
- ✓ a centrepiece on a table for a wedding
- ✓ a sweet, fun baby shower with a colour theme
- ✓ teepees for a kid's party in the back yard
- ✓ a new outfit to make a statement.

For my dinner party, I choose a blue beret and my winter boots to become Madame Gibbs. For Bill, it's a new shirt, a cap and some clumsy French words.

Regardless, a celebration is layered with the elements of happy conversation, unexpected surprises and a gathering of people who are thrown together.

CELEBRATION

Questions to ask yourself

- How can you make a celebration wondrous and personal?
- Will you allow a variety of backgrounds and cultures to be a part of your celebration?
- How can you gather ideas for this event?
- Can you trust your intuition to make the occasion a great event?

Activities to Try

- ✓ Make celebration bunting from scrap materials.
- ✓ Encourage children to host small parties.
- ✓ Buy a big cooler. Set up a drink corner.
- ✓ Encourage storytelling and offer a prize for the worst joke.

seasons

> " Seasons of mists and mellow fruitfulness, close bosom-friend of the maturing sun.
>
> – John Keats

Seasonal cycles are all around us

The changing of the seasons is a beautiful time. Spring flowers are budding in the garden: azaleas, gardenias, camellias and lavender. There's the smell of gums and natives, birds calling, mulberries ripening, the hum of bees, and new blades of grass growing.

It's a different air with runny noses and itchy eyes, but there's more colour in the garden now. Wardrobes change to adjust to the weather patterns. Seasons offer new connections and surprises.

I like the way that seasons define the landscape. Colours change. Shadows shift.

The heart has a quiet voice.

SEASONS

Our lives have seasons too

My heart turns to the season of spring when my daughter prepares for the birth of twins.

She experiences a lot of nausea and tiredness throughout her pregnancy. Her emotions range from shock and concern to fear and happiness. I know she feels overwhelmed. My own emotions range from disbelief and worry to delight and love.

My respect for her grows.

I think of the two hearts beating, the two bodies moving and the two minds developing within her. Every day, she carries within her a promise that her life will change in a big way. For now, though, it's her body shape that is changing.

I'm simply the onlooker, the encourager and support team.

To give her some rest, I take my almost-two-year-old granddaughter, Matilda, for a walk to Misty's coffee shop. It's ten minutes from my daughter's house to a small playground next to a café and hairdresser.

The rich aroma of coffee is in the air.

SEASONS

When I retreat from the chaos, I find connection

Young families gather to meet, play and connect in the playground. It's here that I encounter some new faces.

There are grandmothers pushing children on swings, fathers supervising their toddlers, a family eating brekky, and school students waiting for buses or texting on phones. I find it easy to start conversations based on children's ages or the weather.

Spontaneous interactions add a joy to my day.

At the slippery slide, I meet a family who've moved up from Canberra. I start talking to the mother about her children and, before long, the topic changes to the woman's physical relocation. She talks about her country of birth, Ireland.

I listen to her beautiful accent, and I can picture the distance she's travelled, leaving her family to come to Australia. We're now both supervising children on the swings. Listening to her story is relaxing. I can walk away at any time. She can too. It's an unexpected connection: a different way of thinking about life.

The children's names create a starting point for the conversation, but we say goodbye to each other like we're old friends.

A month later, the season has changed

Time passes and the twins arrive. News of the birth spreads. There's excitement and joy. Newborns Annabel and James are now wrapped up, snug in their twin capsules. They're back from hospital, surrounded by vases of flowers and a doting two-year-old 'big sister' who discovers she likes to pat their heads and tickle their toes.

Matilda insists on more mummy cuddles now that the babies are around. She is curious and helpful. With a new season of love and night-time anxieties, and a towering pile of laundry and emotional adjustments, keeping a toddler happy is important.

Family life can be hectic. Sometimes it's a struggle for everyone to ride the rollercoaster of happy chaos.

SEASONS

The changing seasons always bring newness

As the seasons of life come to us, we may be a dancer on a stage, a climber on a mountain or a parent with babe in arms. There's a season each of innocence and experience, one of maturity and immaturity, one of birth and death, and one of work and play.

Has there been a season of patience and persistence in your life? Perhaps you've connected with the changes in weather, mood and temperament. Or maybe you've connected with friends, family and people from the past.

From spring flowers to winter snow, from productivity to aridness, there are different ways of approaching creativity in all its ripeness and richness.

Creativity welcomes new ideas in all four seasons of the year. It helps us to express new feelings and the passing of time and age.

Sometimes, the seasons transition gradually, like autumn leaves from amber to red. Other times, they're sharp and abrupt, like a thunderstorm that rumbles and cracks in the sky. In both the gradual and sudden changes, creativity is ever-present in our lives.

The Keats image of a close bosom-friend is one to ponder.

Questions to ask yourself

- ✎ When do you mostly notice a shift in seasons?
- ✎ Is there a time for creativity in your neighbourhood?
- ✎ How can you be grateful for the seasons in your life?
- ✎ Do you remember a season of fruitfulness? What happened?

Activities to Try

- ✓ In summer, plunge into the cool ocean and enjoy the salt spray.
- ✓ In autumn, collect leaves and berries out in nature.
- ✓ In winter, cook a minestrone soup.
- ✓ In spring, arrange freshly picked flowers in a vase.

Extra reflection

Seasons of Change

The wonder of the first cry
A time to say goodbye
The heart feels strong.

The connection of long-lost friends
Embracing a smile that never ends
The heart feels love.

The unexpected sense of pride
A renewed joy that we hide
The heart feels peace.

The beauty of a sunrise born
An empty ache to hold and mourn
The heart feels sad.

Seasons come and go
Perhaps some travel slow
The heart feels patience.

M J Gibbs

quietude

> **"** Sometimes you just need a break. In a beautiful place. Alone. To figure everything out.
>
> – Anon

Silence has always been a path to creativity

Silence is important for creativity, wonder and connection to others. It helps to refresh us from the chatter and the 'mind humming' that exists. It allows us to withdraw from the rumble of traffic, the mumbling of shoppers, the ear-splitting music in night clubs and the noisy ephemera around us.

Contemplation in a quiet garden or space to sit and ponder is worth gold. We need silence to savour and wonder, and quietness to connect with ourselves. Meditating and clearing our minds enables our tired bodies to rest.

In *The Art of Effortless Living* (2002), Ingrid Bacci, PhD offers compelling evidence that creative, productive individuals are those who practise effortless living. Her profound guide to making transformative shifts in the body, mind and spirit suggests several ways to discover the freedom of expressing your best self.

And part of doing this, to my thinking, includes taking time to enjoy being quiet.

From a 'hurry sickness' to a quieter rejuvenation, retirees like Bill and I find life in Mapleton right for us.

Quietness feeds our souls, which – in turn – allows us to connect to others.

Contemplation on a train journey

I see the effects of quiet best when it's suddenly gone

Bill and I are passengers on a fast bullet train from Shanghai to Chongqing. We're part of a group of 40 fellow tourists who are on holidays for 21 days.

It's the last part of the tour.

We follow our expert guide, Richard, who capably directs both our luggage and our weary bodies. We find the right carriage on a sparse, clean platform, wheel our suitcases onto the train and find the right places for our luggage to rest. This is no simple feat, especially when the 40 of us fill up four carriages and are spread out with the locals, who'd all booked their places before us.

Eventually, however, we find our seats.

Fortunately, Catherine and her husband, Jan, – who are also on our tour – are sitting directly opposite us. They're not perfect strangers – more newish friends. We make light conversation, exchange the titles of books we're reading and unwrap our sandwiches to eat.

Briefly, we share a drink, and then Bill, Catherine and Jan shut their eyes for the trip. Not me, though. I open my laptop, ready to draw inspiration and work on some writing.

The first part of the journey is quiet. There's a gentle, soothing silence that allows my creative thoughts to flow. I'm relieved that we made it on time and can stop now. Every now and then, I look up from my screen to observe the scenery out the window or glance at people's expressions.

I continue to tap away on my laptop, occasionally looking around, but mostly settling into my focus and concentrating.

Then the peace is disturbed

Abruptly, mobile phones ping, chatter and chime. The woman with the food trolley calls out. It's like a performance on stage.

There's a high-pitched squeal. Talk increases and the sound of the train rattles on. I hear coughs… sneezes… conversations. Catherine is asleep. Bill is softly snoring. Meanwhile, Jan has started reading.

I hear announcements being made: "Dear parents, please do not let your children play or run out of your sight. Thank you for your cooperation," and "Please do not disturb other passengers."

I reflect that when there's quietude, I need to make the most of it. I need to let the peaceful 'shhh' of those moments sing to me. If I'm confined to a seat in a train carriage across from a stranger, I need to politely let them know that I need to not talk.

We need silence to meditate. It feeds the creative part of us that's necessary to connect to others later.

QUIETUDE

Silence creates a 'margin' of space in our lives

Silence can be a cooperation between you and another person, whether on a train, a plane, a bus or at home. A meaningful silence is always better than meaningless words.

That train trip in China lasts seven hours. After conversations, sleeping, eating and quietude, Bill and I finally arrive at our destination, weary but ready for the next adventure. We enjoy a good night's sleep in a hotel, tucked beneath comfortable, clean sheets.

10 Things Every Parent Needs to Know (2018) by psychologist and educator Dr Justin Coulson, PhD is an excellent book for all parents. In it, he says:

Slow down, sit quietly, be available, and create 'margin' in your life. Margin is that space on the page where there is room for notes and connection. Margin is that space in our lives where there is room for other people and the possibility of change.
I know for myself that I can't be creative with a head full of external noise and distractions.

Only with silence around me can my inner ideas bloom.

QUIETUDE

Questions to ask yourself

- When does silence motivate you?
- Do you make time for quietness?
- What do you think about when you're silent?
- How does a lack of noise affect you?
- What books have you read that encourage a quieter lifestyle?

Activities to Try

- ✓ Look at the following photos. Find a comfortable place to sit still and admire the colours, textures, patterns and shapes.

- ✓ Listen to quiet instrumental music and close your eyes.
- ✓ Challenge yourself with a silent meditation. Add it to the week's activities. Listen to a meditation on the Calm app or try Headspace.
- ✓ Consider doing a silent retreat with no internet, phone, music or communication with people for a few days.
- ✓ Speak these words from Rabindranath Tagore (2004): "God's silence ripens man's thoughts into speech."

empathy

> " Empathy is about standing in someone else's shoes, feeling with his or her heart, seeing with his or her eyes. Not only is empathy hard to outsource and automate, but it makes the world a better place.
>
> – Daniel Pink

Empathy is inextricably tied to connection

I think that empathy is our most undervalued and untapped resource, because it's the place where our feelings and emotions are transformed.

Connecting to others' feelings means cultivating empathy.

Risk, vulnerability, understanding: they're things I strive to attain, even though a critical voice emerges at times to spoil it. But by cultivating empathetic skills, I can learn to improve and sustain healthy connections with others.

Well, this is my wish, anyway.

Sympathy is feeling compassion, sorrow or pity for the hardships that another person encounters, but empathy is putting yourself in their shoes.

That's why actors often talk about empathy.

EMPATHY

Opportunities for empathy are everywhere

Arriving back in Brisbane from our holiday in China, Bill and I catch the train from the Brisbane Airport to Nambour via Caboolture. Can you imagine our joy to be going home as we look out the train window at a clear, blue, beautiful sky?

A tall, slim, fidgety man wearing faded jeans and a black t-shirt jumps into the carriage. He sits next to me and asks us where we've been travelling. The suitcases are a clue, and the conversation starts. He reminds me of my eldest son and, when he introduces himself, I discover that – by chance – he's also an Andrew (my son's name).

I notice that this Andrew seems restless, edgy and talkative. It turns out that he's going through a break-up with his long-time girlfriend, and is feeling very lost and agitated. He's on his way to a Buddhist retreat at Eudlo, where he plans to volunteer, recover, shut the world out and disappear.

Conversations with Strangers

He tells me that he's sold all his possessions, and is dealing with mental instability and loneliness.

Empathy is something Andrew needs

The conversation develops very freely between Andrew and me. It's not what I expect from returning home to Mapleton. Nor does it turn into the conversation of complex heartbreak that I think it's going to. I don't have the best energy for it – and yet it calls me, so I respond.

Bill's sitting on the opposite side, nodding off to sleep.

I listen to Andrew as his story unfolds. It's a serendipitous moment. He's stuck, sad and at risk of harming himself. His friends don't think he'll last a week in the retreat. He tells me that his parents disowned him long ago due to his drug problems. His life seems empty.

He looks as though he's recently lost weight, his eyes seem soulless and a frown creases his forehead.

I listen as he tells me more of his story. I promise that I'll contact him after a week to see how he's going. He gives me his mobile number, says goodbye and jumps off the train with his slightly hunched shoulders.

I gaze out at the sun-drenched sky.

Talking with Andrew provides me with a wonderful opportunity

Some might think of a stranger in his late thirties approaching them as a problem, rather than as a remarkable opportunity to learn, grow and show empathy. But instead of ignoring him, I embrace this opportunity to hear out his troubles.

As I do, I learn a lot about his background, values and failures. This train connection challenges me to be sensitive and think about other people's situations. I make it my business to listen and understand his hurts.

I don't focus on whether there's a creative solution to his problems.

And when I follow up with him a week later, he thanks me for thinking of him.

EMPATHY

So much of empathy comes down to listening

The skill of active listening can be incredibly useful in developing empathy.

This involves pausing the inner chatter of your own thoughts to listen thoughtfully to the other person's words. You need to avoid jumping in and cutting the person off mid-sentence. Then you need to repeat what they've said back to them in a slightly different way to acknowledge their ideas.

This is not always something that's been easy for me to do.

While my parents taught me kindness, creativity and responsibility, I didn't always empathise with others – especially when I was a self-absorbed teenager at university. Back then, I was too busy telling everyone else my own opinions or thoughts.

Yet, in their unique ways, my parents both set examples of creativity and empathy for me. My father was a carpenter and my mother, a seamstress. Both were skilled at using their hands and both were creative individuals.

As I grew up, I watched them write, build, sew and renovate. As they did, they both allowed others into their home without prior invitation. This generous spirit, in turn, allowed for surprising, bold conversations that connected them to a diverse range of people.

And from home and my parents, I learnt and developed skills in empathy.

EMPATHY

Questions to ask yourself

- ✎ Do you cultivate a heart for empathy?
- ✎ Is there someone you know who needs help?
- ✎ How can you bring happiness to a sad situation?
- ✎ Are you sensitive to others from different backgrounds? Why?
- ✎ What can you offer to others that brings joy to them?

Activities to Try

- ✓ Visit a friend's workplace and take the opportunity to notice their routine and work.
- ✓ Look at a friend's Instagram page to observe their creativity.
- ✓ Write a few choice words on a card to make a difference on an anniversary.
- ✓ Listen with your heart for compassion and understanding, not problem-solving.
- ✓ Make a new connection in your street.

food

> " Food brings people together on many different levels. It's nourishment of the soul and body; it's truly love.
>
> – Giada De Laurentiis

Food fuels both connection and creativity

Summer in Mapleton brings ripe fruits, balmy lunches and dreamy backyard barbecues with Bill's favourite: a rib eye fillet sizzling on the grill. Toss in some onions, sweet potatoes and mushrooms, add a crispy, green salad, and this brings about a lazy, magical evening watching the sun set out over the sea.

Bill likes to say, "What you eat today walks and talks tomorrow."

There's a profound meaning to our lives when it comes to eating and wellbeing. Enjoying good food is certainly a pleasure. Our travels have taught us that conversations with strangers commonly centre on what's on our plates.

The topic makes for great connection and allows us to enhance our creativity – for example, by comparing recipes with each other. There's a group knowledge that we can tap into around the dinner table that might just extend our creative juices.

It becomes a shared synthesis of new ideas that leads to a completely different way of doing things.

FOOD

A French cooking school – Maubec en Luberon

It's not often that you get to meet a group of total strangers who come together to learn French cuisine. Even less often does it happen in the heart of wonderful Provence.

Tucked away in the countryside of the Luberon National Park, you'll find Jean-Marc and Alice's charming Provencal-style home in the village of Maubec. It's full of style and in a dream location. As I arrive, I'm warmly welcomed by the lovely Alice, who serves me and the others coffee and homemade madeleines.

I appreciate the chance to chat with the new guests and learn more about them.

The opportunities for connection are immediate

I meet Tuula: an American married to a Frenchman who lives in Toulon. There's also Kleah and Gerry from Colorado, Denver, who are married with no kids. And there's Kiyomi from Tokyo, herself a chef, who's very shy and speaks little English. And finally, of course, there's moi!

Together, we make up a group of possibilities: culinary creatives who connect with each other over new ingredients, different techniques and an enthusiasm for tasting. We unite in our red aprons with recipes and utensils, a few mistakes and a keenness to support one another.

The kitchen is designed to teach hands-on French cooking, and it lets us practise near the chef. We benefit from his advice and expertise, learning new skills.

Firstly, Jean-Marc takes us to the Petit Palais farmer's market

At the outdoor market, we purchase a basket, and everyone gets to taste-test the various offerings. It's all fresh and delicious.

Then we hop back into our cars and head to the kitchen. A sense of friendliness and ease follows on from the light conversation, questions and mingling at the market. We all come from different backgrounds, family

situations and cultures, but we're here to learn and experiment the French way.

Jean-Marc is a wonderful teacher and organiser who speaks perfect English and is good-humoured too. There's a three-course gastronomic menu ('amuses-bouches' plus two dishes and a dessert). It also includes wines, teas and coffees.

Connection, creativity and ooh la lahhs!

Can you smell the sea bass on fresh garlic puree with green olives, fava beans and sage sauce?

Perhaps you can bite down on the shortbread cookie with real strawberry jam, flavoured with lemon verbena and sorbet? Or can you mix the dough in a bowl with powdered sugar, flour and baking powder with lemon zest? And can you taste the goat cheese cromesquis with asparagus and mixed green salad?

Mmm. It's all delicious!

As we reach the end of our cooking duties, we step out onto the sunny terrace, overlooking the Luberon mountains. Alice has dressed the table beautifully. Over a glass of champagne, this amazing connection of strangers comes easily, amicably and without barriers. It's born of cooperation, teamwork and a mutual joy in food.

In between dishes, we share stories and generally marvel at the gratitude we feel at enjoying such a lovely day together. Tuula and I really click after we discover that we both write blogs. I'm fascinated by how she left America to start up her new life, and we connect online too.

Over the course of a single day, our international rapport has grown from a beginning as strangers to a meaningful friendship.

FOOD

Food fosters further connections and friendship

To increase connection between strangers, food becomes a warm-hearted way to share stories from the past, present and future.

Often, in a comfortable setting, the pleasure of eating with others allows for memories to come and find their homes in people's hearts. Food tastes better. Conversations emerge. Emotions surface.

A fine glass of champagne unites and celebrates others during the course of the evening. The creativity grows from these opportunities in problem-solving and discussion over a delicious meal.

These connections bring gratitude and joy, health and happiness.

FOOD

Questions to ask yourself

- What foods or drinks make it easier to connect?
- How can you best show creativity around the table, restaurant or café scene?
- When do you most feel connected to food and others?
- When do you feel most creative regarding food? Why?

Activities to Try

- ✓ Cook for friends or invite strangers to your home.
- ✓ Order something different at a café that you haven't tried before.
- ✓ Consider hosting a Christmas party to connect with past friends.
- ✓ Try a cooking class in a rural location, farm or vineyard.

Conversations with Strangers

Love

> " Love is patient. Love is kind. Love isn't jealous. It doesn't sing its own praises. It isn't arrogant. It isn't rude. It doesn't think about itself. Love isn't irritable. It doesn't keep track of wrongs. It isn't happy when injustice is done, but it is happy with the truth. Love never stops being patient, never stops believing, never stops hoping, never gives up.
>
> – 1 Corinthians 13, 4-8,
>   God's Word translation

We all need a little love...

Love is a word that sums up what we all need and desire.

But there are many different kinds: love of family, love of self, love of friends, love of God and love of life. Intimate connection to others enables love to grow.

Love acknowledges the other person. As Paul the Apostle wrote in the above quote, it isn't self-seeking.

I keep coming back to love when the challenges and struggles in life test me.

One of the first gifts Bill gives me on a romantic date is a book called *Gift from the Sea* by Anne Morrow Lindbergh. It is graceful, lucid and lyrical. It shares the author's meditations on youth and age, love and marriage, peace, solitude and contentment as she set them down during a brief vacation by the sea.

Inside the cover, Bill writes:

My one true love,

May your life be lived in grace, and joy your constant companion. Thank you for the awakening.

Yours always, Bill.

This little book allows me to escape from the same-sameness of my everyday rituals to find contemplation and creativity within my life.

LOVE

Love and creativity can both come in many shapes

Bill and I take a drive to Palmwoods, a rural town in the Sunshine Coast region, to enjoy a coffee and browse the shops.

Close to our car park is a railway goods shed. Inside, it's full of old wares: repurposed furniture, rustic birdhouses, vintage lanterns, scrubbed pine tables and quirky accessories. It's a place of a visual softness that comes from scuffs, bumps and bangs. In it, we see country treasures from gardening supplies to crates and tools.

It is also a place to eat and drink.

This little love date is about spending time together and having light-hearted conversations while immersing ourselves in the visual attractions of the handmade.

Love shines through the quirkiness of upcycled bras

At the back of the shed, I see the most amazing hats. The assistant, Leah, smiles and tells me the story behind her creative designs.

She makes original hats and fascinators from recycled bras and adds lace, buttons and beads. She explains the process of thinking up each idea and how it leads her to source the materials from op shops and then put each hat together.

The creative in me is fascinated by this wonderful idea.

Bill walks towards us. I try on some hats, and the romance starts. Bill tells me I look gorgeous in the red one. Leah comments that her favourite one is bigger, to match her size. She points out one on the top crate, then hands it to me and I try it on.

LOVE

Creativity and love intertwine in Leah's handiwork

The hat Leah points out isn't quite right for me. Still, I twirl around, catching a glimpse of myself in the mirror, and Bill moves closer to give me a kiss. It's a fun type of foreplay.

In the end, I purchase a hat to give to my sister for her birthday.

This 'shop' might be an old shed with timber walls and rugged, recycled cupboards and shelves, but it speaks clearly to us of Leah's creative spark. And it's just an added bonus when she tells us her alias is Steampunk Nellie.

It's also a bonus when Bill and I share a chocolate muffin, enjoying the smell of richly brewed coffee against the backdrop of rockabilly designs. Plus, of course, it's a bonus that I get to model the fascinator I buy for my sister.

Creativity comes in all shapes and sizes, even D-sized bra cups.

LOVE

Love has so many facets...

When it comes to sensory experiences, I love the damp smell of rain in the air, the taste of juicy red plums, the texture and scent of crème caramel and the touch of fine silk on my skin.

I sometimes experience love in the beauty of a gold, glistening sunset or the purple wisteria as it drapes over a pergola. Other times, I see it within the beautiful green peridot in my engagement ring.

Love can always be found in actions: both doing and showing. I feel it when Bill makes me a baked cheesecake, in the embrace and rhythm of a dance, and in a well-told story that pulls at my heartstrings.

In the garden, I love hydrangea blossoms – the big, bluish-tinged-with-green kind that remind me of my childhood home. That's a nostalgic love, interwoven with memories of growing up and hiding in the bushes along the side of my parents' home.

Love can be open and transparent like a new stranger coming into your life. It can be charged with unexpected creativity that widens a view so that you can connect to another. Love has a language all of its own.

It encompasses many feelings – joy, peace and excitement, yet fear, hurt and risk-taking too.

As Helen Keller said, "The best and most beautiful things in the world cannot be seen or even heard but must be felt with the heart."

LOVE

117

Questions to ask yourself

- What's the most important thing for you when it comes to love?
- How does a person transform hate into love?
- Why do you love your family?
- Who else do you love and admire? Why?
- What is your love language? If you're not sure what this term means, check out *The 5 Love Languages* by Gary Chapman.

Activities to Try

- ✓ Make a heart-shaped cake or heart bunting.
- ✓ Write a love message to someone.
- ✓ Compose a love song.
- ✓ Read a book of love poems.
- ✓ Plan a meaningful outing with someone you care about.

art

> " I adore art. The light and colours go to a deeper plane, energizing my creative and feeling life. Art is the shifting from summer white wines to reds and a different heart space.
>
> – Del Kathryn Barton

The link between art and creativity is intuitive

Because I'm a bit of an art addict, I can connect with others while enjoying creativity in galleries, exhibitions, libraries and other places where art is valued. I'm a collector of Indigenous paintings, a reader of artists, a dabbler in collage and a keeper of children's picture books.

Creativity has been consistent in all areas of my life, but particularly in the enjoyment of art. From the time I could first draw, I copied things, pasted pictures and made art. I experimented with painting in watercolours, acrylics and oils.

My father used to keep a canvas I painted when I was 16. He loved the landscape I created using a palette knife. To my surprise, Dad framed my art and hung it in the bedroom.

He made me feel that I was an artist.

Like strangers in all parts of the world, art is everywhere.

I see it on bridges, in factories, and in arcades, shopping malls, home studios and festivals. It's there in children's picture books, on highways and in hotels.

Art has so many types of movements and genres: utopia art, expressionism, cubism, pop art, impressionism, botanical art, cartoons, portraits, landscapes and more.

Desert art has transformed the art landscape of Australia, from Arnhem Land, Torres Straits to Papunya and across to the Kimberley and the West. Across the country, collections of paintings, fibre art, weaving, ghost net baskets and printmaking deserve great recognition and admiration.

Like others who come face to face with you, art can stand out with its bold strokes, textures, colours and capacity to stir emotions.

"Look at me!" it cries. "What do you think of me?"

Art allows people to connect with each other

My connection starts in a street art gallery

On a trip to Yandina near Mapleton, I wander through the Stevens Street art gallery. There, I'm surrounded by abstract paintings, linocuts, woven baskets and wavy, dot-like drawings. I speak to a few people, including a lady who used to run a gallery in Kenilworth.

Her passion for art rubs off onto me as we talk about her recent works on display.

It continues with an interior designer

Later, I find myself entering a pop-up shop, and start a lovely conversation with the owner, Samantha. Sam specialises in interior design. Her small shop space is inspired by a vintage picture that she once found at an op shop. From this picture, she created her entire colour scheme.

I listen to her story. She's Melbourne-born. However, after raising a family and going through a marriage breakdown, she journeyed to Queensland to do what she'd always wanted to do: start up a business. She shows me some of her 'before and after' renovation photographs.

And it helps me to connect with my younger self

From her collection, I remember artistic things I did as a child, and we talk about that. Art speaks to us both. Sam says she never gets bored in the little shop because there's a window that lets her look out onto the street. Through it, she watches the passing cars, people and dogs.

Then, right before our eyes, an old, red car pulls into a car park. The hippie owner gets out with his two poodles on a lead, and we watch, entranced. The fun of having her own 'picture theatre' in front of her keeps her constantly entertained. She delights in the unexpected everyday scenes it shows her.

Gladness and creativity roll into one within her.

ART

How could art help YOU to connect?

Consider your own experience with art. Small efforts can bring big benefits. Much as you'd simply open a door for someone, try asking a question about a painting or complimenting a fellow viewer.

Art has a way of beautifying something, celebrating the skills of another.

Does art move you to feel something? To connect with someone?

Today, meet art where it's at. Meet it in the different backgrounds and cultures of the world. Embrace it as a new language, learning and joy. There should be no desire to add anything, take anything away or change any part.

Art is humanistic and individualistic, just like the anonymous, unfamiliar person in our lives.

ART

Questions to ask yourself

- 🖉 If you painted one picture, what would it be?
- 🖉 Can you draw a still life picture – perhaps a chair, vase or bottle?
- 🖉 Have you viewed any of the many different types of Asian or African art? What did you notice in it?
- 🖉 What do the symbols in Indigenous Australian paintings you've viewed mean?
- 🖉 Has art ever freed you from a reclusive life to an emotionally charged one?

Activities to Try

- ✓ Stencil fruit and vegetable designs onto paper.
- ✓ Use children's drawings to make gift cards.
- ✓ Sketch an object from a high vantage point.
- ✓ Look through art books in a gallery store.
- ✓ Watch a YouTube clip on how to do watercolours, pastels or cartoons.
- ✓ Draw your self-portrait.

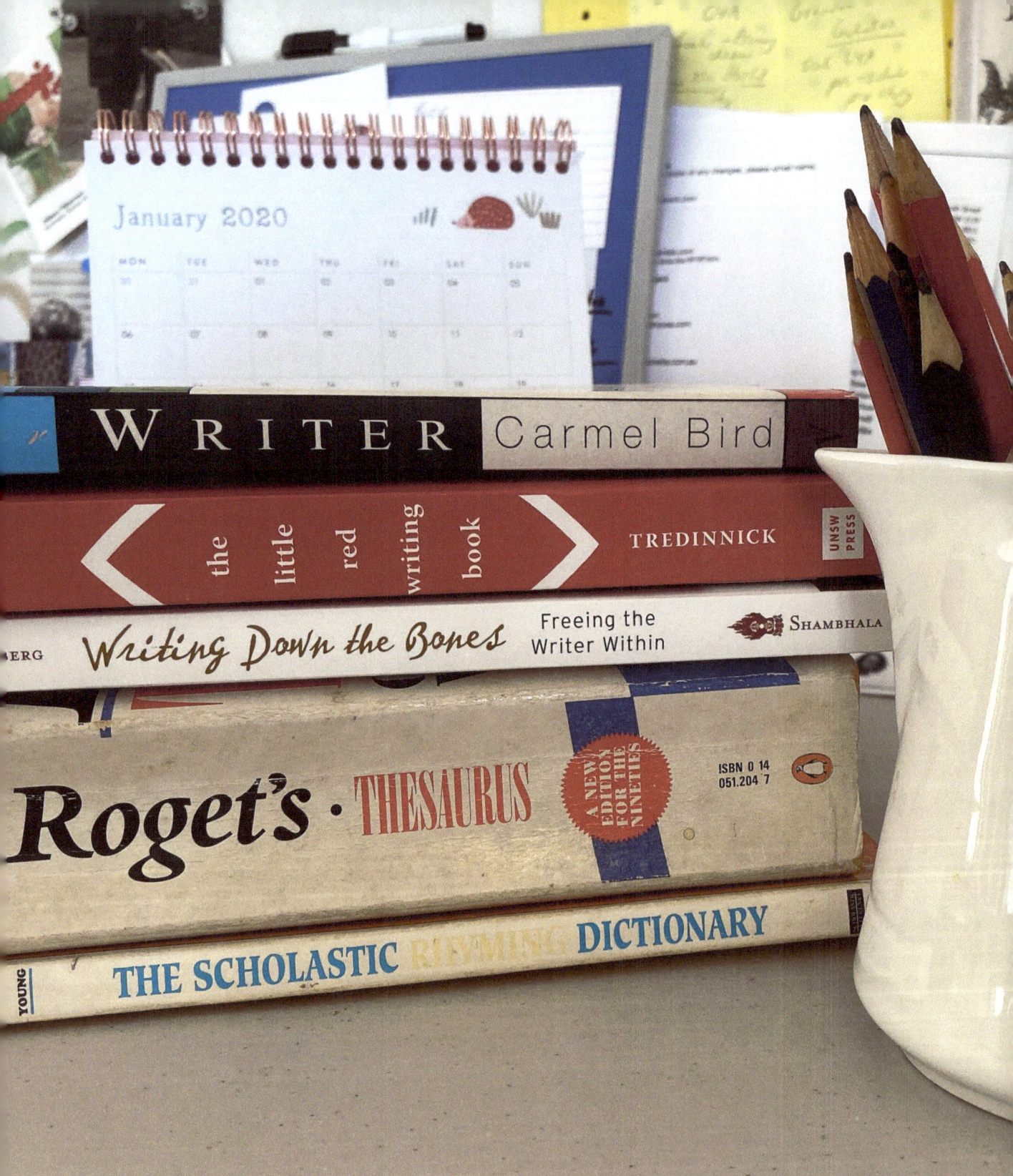

writing

> " A word after a word after a word is power.
>
> – Margaret Atwood

Writing is a doorway to new worlds

A thick fog descends over the mountain in Mapleton, extending right out to the sea. The valley looks like it's a blanket rolling out to the horizon. There's a chill in the air. April brings rain – excessive rain sometimes – and even cyclones up north.

If I can't work out in the garden, my time indoors is productive with writing and reading. Writing, somewhat reflexively, allows me to think about why I love to write. I love to express emotions. To clarify things. To explore. To be creative and connect with others. If I have something to say, I write it down.

Writing opens up new windows to different worlds.

It enriches my life.

Meanwhile, reading what other people have written is also a pathway for me to visit wonderful worlds. It provides imagination, discernment, pleasure and relaxation.

The power of other people's writing engages all my senses.

Without the play of words, the taste loses its flavour. I chew and chew, edit and edit. I pop the gum, reach the climax, spit the gum out and send the manuscript off.

Different flavours of gum, different genres of writing.

The wordsmith in me captures something that I can turn into meaning. Blogging creatively keeps me connected with others.

Reading offers another

The reader in me nourishes creativity and extends the connection to others.

Reading other people's writing is also a golden treasure that challenges, extends and empowers me, bringing me understanding and wisdom. Reading involves pacing myself, discovering, anticipating, realising and making connections.

Writing and reading can both be forms of meditation.

Both rely on cognitive processes and each helps the other.

Writing offers one kind of treasure...

When I write, I'm often surprised. Writing is a path to meeting and becoming intimate with myself.

I realise in this moment that writing is like a chewing gum treasure. It stretches me. It sticks to me and tastes tangy. When I've had enough, though, I spit it out.

Writing connects me with a friend in London

Writing to a dear friend who lives on the other side of the world has its strong foundations in my primary school days.

We started off as strangers, sitting in classrooms at Graceville Primary School. We discovered shared interests and Christian values, and developed a connection that has grown over 50 years. Now married with three grown-up children who live around the world, Dallas corresponds with me from London where she currently lives.

She's an international traveller with a heart of gold.

I experience joy every time we write to each other

I know surprises always await me in the mail. Like the time she sent me a note that said:

> I can't find any notepaper in this apartment at all. I wanted to send you these cards I collected in London for you. They all reminded me of you in one way or another. We're currently in Melbourne but head to Brisbane tomorrow.

This written act of kindness has a ripple effect

My relationship with Dallas is a mutually beneficial one that helps me grow. If you're reaching out to a random stranger, on the other hand, find out what their passions, skills and interests are. Be respectful and polite, putting yourself in their shoes.

I've learnt to consider others and their passions when I post something in the mail, write a blog or interview, or even communicate on Instagram.

This bond I have with Dallas is better suited to long-term friendships than conversations with complete strangers. However, a conversation with some unknown person may prompt you to meet up again with them.

If the connection is very good, you might offer a card you've written, give a small token of appreciation or pay for the coffee. I think this is part of caring for others: remembering their favourite song, colour, author or book. Yet many people leave surprise handwritten notes for strangers to uplift and support them.

I wonder what difference it makes to their lives when they read the right words on a page.

In the parcel, there are ten greeting cards that are beautiful both in artistic design and written message. There are owls, penguins, puffins, and images from stories like the Mad Hatter's Tea Party, The Owl and the Pussycat, and The Tortoise and the Hare.

These mostly contain children's illustrations. Dallas found them in art galleries, museums or boutique gift shops in London. She's done her homework and knows me well. It's a carefully considered collection, and I love the cards. Her thoughtful words touch me.

Once again, creativity and connection spark joy for me.

Together, reading and writing bring joy

Both actively writing and reading other people's words can create a spontaneous connection. This can involve creative story-writing, poetry and sharing words with others. It might involve going deeper into the heart, mind and spirit of a person.

Perhaps writing can also offer encouragement and good cheer to others. And reading can offer solace, escape, comfort and healing.

For me, both reading and writing allow for reflection.

Writing orders my life, and reading colours in the spaces.

Small writing treasures drop down from different places and, like chewing gum, they stick. A phrase, story or sentiment written in a greeting card can communicate wonders.

Golden treasures pile up and, like precious gems, they sparkle and shine.

Questions to ask yourself

- When was the last time you wrote or read something profound?
- Do you journal? If so, how often?
- Where is a place that you can write or read comfortably?
- What would you write or read if you had only hours to live?
- What memories do you cherish most from your childhood?

Activities to Try

- ✓ Write a letter to your future self.
- ✓ Write an apology to someone you've hurt.
- ✓ Write about the things that you're looking forward to.
- ✓ Read *Writing Down the Bones: Freeing the Writer Within* by Natalie Goldberg.
- ✓ Listen to www.onemorepagepodcast.com (for lovers of kid's books).

The joy of journaling

Ah! The sweet mysteries and secrets that lie hidden on paper in our personal history and the world's narratives. Many wonderful experiences have been recorded by famous diarists through their words: Anne Frank, Virginia Woolf, Katherine Mansfield and Agatha Christie.

As Alyss Thomas says in *The Journal Writer's Companion* (2019):

> *A journal is the private space where you believe in your ideas and your unformed, unknown thoughts. Your journal is where you can be the best version of you that is still in the process of being discovered, where you know you're going to be the best at what you do, and where you are prepared to work away until your projects, your ideas, or your … sense of self are robust enough to be seen in public.*

Bonus writing activity

Mix and match the terms in the following table, add some conflict and dialogue, and come up with an interesting story. Then throw into the mix a stranger who adds intrigue and mystery. Voila! Give your characters unique names and personalities.

(Conflict could include getting lost, accidents, sickness, theft or an earthquake.)

Characters

- Cyclist
- Doctor
- Taxi driver
- Blind man
- Child
- Male masseur
- Female scientist
- Girl

Actions

- Horse riding
- Tai chi
- Skateboarding
- Dancing
- Crying
- Climbing
- Sleeping
- Painting

Place

- Chinese museum
- Tehran bazaar
- Italian café
- Mountains in New Zealand
- Dublin street
- Paris restaurant
- African safari
- Sydney park

Extra reflection

The Magic Hand

Writing, the forever friend
who holds you while you shake;
the storyteller
with words that echo into the night
Light.

Writing, the cherished friend
who asks about your soul;
the listener
with open ear
Fear.

Writing, the secret friend
who walks with you;
the lover
whose tickle and tease
Please.

Writing, the spiritual friend
who contemplates;
the traveller
eyes to see the sky
WHY?

M J Gibbs

goals

❝ A goal is not always meant to be reached. It often serves simply as something to aim at.

– Bruce Lee

The end of the year brings the possibility of new goals

At the beginning of each year, I try to set goals for myself.

To help me, I buy an attractive calendar and journal. I love the smell and feel of a new diary. This year, the beautiful *Twigseeds Diary* by Kate Knapp is a gift to myself that's filled with inspirational quotes.

Its crisp, clean pages combine quirky, whimsical illustrations with spaces to write important dates, events and birthdays. Filling it out with reminders of days that are significant to people I care about is a creative act that connects me to them.

Setting goals feels right at the start of a new year because it helps me to focus on my priorities, such as family. It's a simple, positive step to make things that matter – like planning a trip away – happen. It also helps me to move beyond the same-sameness of my everyday routine.

When I set goals, I feel more confident about making bold decisions that bring healthy balance to my life.

Specific goals often change from year to year

An example of a yearly goal for me might be to walk daily or to help others more. I also include personal goals like:

- ✓ running a marathon (hasn't happened yet!)
- ✓ completing a university degree (yes)
- ✓ finishing a patchwork quilt or writing a children's book (currently doing both).

At home, I set goals for myself in the garden to manage water restrictions and to be more alert to the presence of snakes and jumping ants. I need to wear boots and cover up my arms, pay more attention to the red soil and step carefully on uneven ground.

This year, I set a goal to garden as part of my everyday routine. I decide to devote a small section of time daily to planting, pruning and weeding. For me, this is about experiencing more joyful moments.

It's about being grateful.

But goal-setting can also be about taking risks, improving oneself and helping others.

For many people, that means connecting with their own tribe, whoever that may be.

Creative solutions to a community clean-up

Visiting the Montville Pharmacy, I meet a woman from Yamba in New South Wales.

Carole Anne is a perfect stranger to me, but as we wait together at the counter to purchase our products, she mentions that she's made Flaxton her home for the past ten weeks. During our conversation, she talks about a terrible storm she experienced back in Yamba. She describes how the locals rallied together to mend roofs and fix fences after the storm wreaked its havoc.

I immediately remember the time my parents' house went under in the Brisbane flood. The stench of mud, the weight of the water and the massive clean-up afterwards remain vivid in my memories. Carole Anne's recollection is similar – the shock, panic, devastation and need to get back on your feet again.

Now, she tells me, she's starting over again after eight years of living in New South Wales. I don't expect to connect so easily to her story, yet it instantly takes me back to the way in which the Brisbane deluge impacted my family and their community.

After a frightening natural disaster, people rally together with the shared goal of helping and caring for each other. Neighbours come together to check the damage, fix things, move furniture, wash clothes and retrieve precious personal items.

I remember that the immediate goal for my family was to clean up the mud, mess and rubble after the 'big wet'. The community goal was one of compassion and kindness. Both goals were useful – and both were needed.

Both allowed creative solutions to come with hard work and problem-solving.

GOALS

Goals can bring a sense of purpose and connection

Goals help you to navigate the priorities in your life.

So if greater connection is one of your priorities, goals can help you to make it happen.

Goals prepare your thoughts, feelings and spirit to take positive steps and make bold decisions. They direct your path away from the same-sameness to imagine and aim for new opportunities. And while I like to set goals at the beginning of the year, it's never too late to set and then work towards them.

Sharing this book is one goal I've put into action. With it, I hope to motivate you to linger a little with strangers and start interesting conversations that bring you joy, spontaneity and fun.

GOALS

Questions to ask yourself

- What is your goal for the week? For the year?
- Is there a creative friend you can share your goals with?
- How often do you examine your goals to see if they're still relevant?
- Are you honest about your short-term and long-term goals?

Activities to Try

- ✓ Practise SMART goals (Google this).
- ✓ Plan two short-term goals for this week.
- ✓ Be accountable to a friend for your goals.
- ✓ Reach out to someone who's creative and practical, and who understands the value of goal-setting.

Extra reflection

The Hope Tree

A seed
Timely washed and renewed with rain
Soon a green shoot grows
Bursting through the air like a mighty warrior
Proud, fierce, strong.

Where there was death
A chance of life.

Across the burnt and stricken land
Of black trees and scarred hills
Cracked earth and sweaty rocks
Blistering sky
Grows a tree that has won the battle.

The hope tree lives on.

M J Gibbs

Sometimes, goals need to be changed

On my way back from the shops at Noosaville, I meet a woman with two toddlers in a stroller. One is 2½ years and the other is 18 months. She tells me she's struggling as a single parent, and we talk about support systems for raising children alone.

The short-term goal of helping to mind the children to give her some respite nudges me. But I can't solve her problems and nor do I wish to interfere. So, instead, I change my goal to one of encouragement and offer her a hug. She tells me it's a blessing, and her teary smile stays with me for a few days. In this situation, changing my goal brings both compassion and connection.

final musings

By now, I hope you see how talking with strangers can enrich your life

In my own life, I see it as a privilege to share creativity and connection with someone I've never met. I realise, however, that the thought of this might challenge you, especially if you're scared of talking to strangers.

But, as I've mentioned a few times throughout this book, there's a same-sameness to our daily routines of life that can entrap us. It's a predictable way of doing things that most of us like to hold onto.

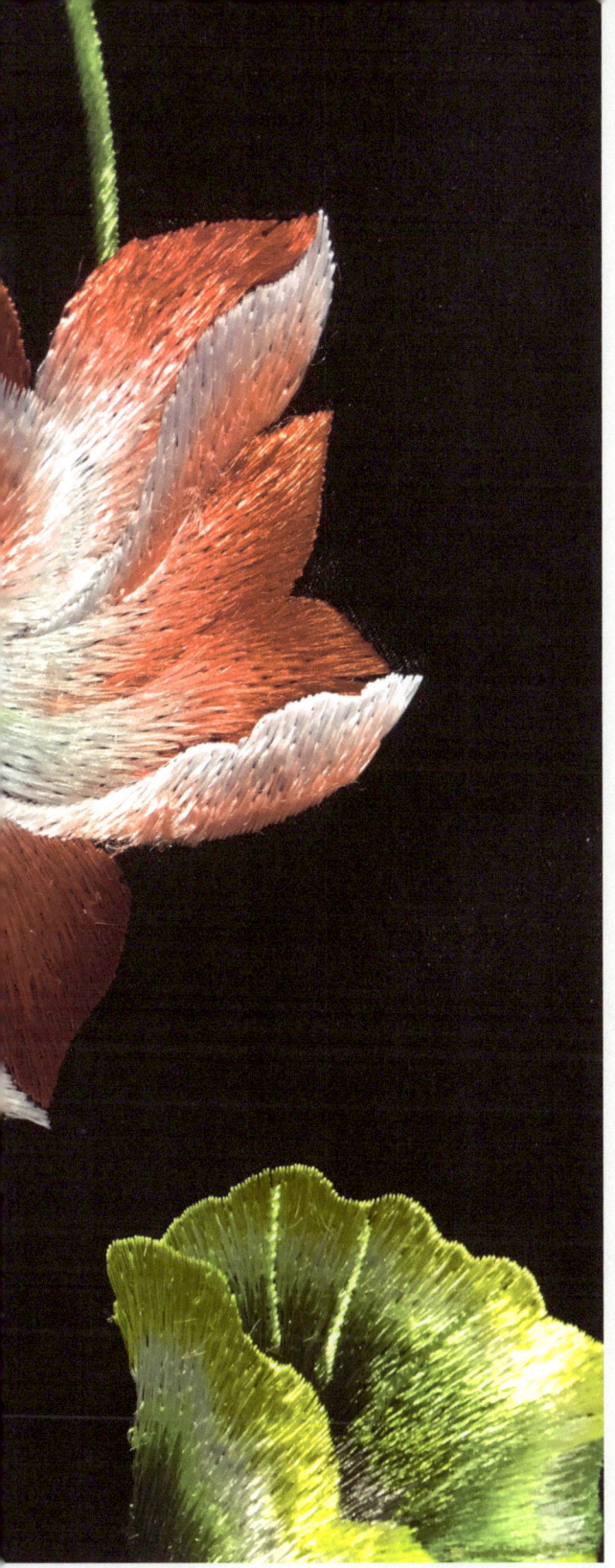

And either we feel like we lose ourselves in it, or we become bored or uncertain of life's journey. Then, suddenly, something kicks in to challenge this. It might be a new adventure, a new purpose to travel or an unexpected crisis that pulls us in a different direction.

I've experienced all of these things through my conversations with strangers.

You can, too, if you're open to new connections that bring creativity and spontaneity.

Where could your new-found creativity take you?

Throughout this book, you've joined me in exploring new seasons, miraculous love and blossoming friendships. You've savoured moments of quietude in nature and shared splendid memories of travel. You've celebrated creative pursuits like writing, art and the culinary delights of good food.

You've also seen how food can lead to exciting conversations around a table with others sharing their stories. And you've seen how travel can take you from where you are to where you could go.

Beyond this, you've explored memories of beloved childhood things, ways to show empathy and gratitude for goals you've set. You've discovered how a walk in nature can awaken a desire to relax into easier conversation. You've also learnt how that conversation can then bring a mutual understanding with others.

Perhaps the themes in the chapters remind you of your own life's perspectives, goals and emotions. Maybe they inspire you with how love can transform your stuck ways to build bridges that connect you with other people's cultures, ideas and dreams.

So now, if anything in this book has inspired you, I'd love you to consider reading my blog www.themoderngrandmasmanual.com.au. It's all about creativity, connection and community.

I don't know if I've reached wisdom, but I hope that my experiences will help to spark meaningful interaction and connection with others for you. One of the benefits of getting older is recognising that there are so many moments of richness and beauty in life.

It's my fondest wish that telling you my experiences with honesty in my heart will inspire you and others to live joyously.

Cheers and love

Marg Gibbs

FINAL MUSINGS

Acknowledgements

Firstly, I'd like to thank my daughter, Rachael, for the concise phrase she used in a card to me for my 60th birthday. She's one of my golden treasures and inspires me to be the person I am.

Next, to my brother, Jim, and sister, Kim, who know me well, make mistakes along the way with me and love me. Thank you for the beautiful childhood memories that we share.

Thanks also to my friends Shannyn McSweeney and Dallas Buckley who, in their wisdom and compassion, encourage me with writing to spread my wings.

Thank you to my three sons, Andrew, Lachie and Tim, along with my extended family, who enrich my connections with others.

To my Mapleton community and friends: I owe you gratitude for the many ways you've included me in the town. You're also responsible for my commitment to, and passion for, writing.

To Alex Fullerton, Sylvie Blair and Natasha Higgins: thanks for the patience, understanding and guidance through the hard work of creating a book. I've valued and appreciated your feedback. And to Tanja Gardner in New Zealand: thanks for the sharp, brilliant editing mind that's supported me through the process of writing this book.

To Dr Mark Gibbs, whose name I bear: thank you for your unwavering support over many decades.

Thanks to my soul mate, friend and husband, Bill Smith, whose prose, poetry and wisdom have been invaluable in my Mapleton journey. Thanks for the breathing space to maintain the book's momentum. I deeply respect your listening ear, your generous, creative spirit, your love and your spiritual connection.

Finally, I'd like to acknowledge God, my creative sustainer and One who draws me closer to Him.

Want to continue the conversation?

If you've enjoyed the journey through these pages with me, I invite you to continue the conversation by reading my blog. You can find that at www.themoderngrandmasmanual.com.au.

Perhaps in the future, you might consider taking a course with me to explore your creativity further. To discover what's on offer, visit my website www.mjgibbs.com.au.

And if you'd simply like to stay connected, there's always social media. Follow me on:

- ✓ Instagram – @marg_gibbs
- ✓ Facebook – @marg.gibbs.921

In the meantime, enjoy the moments of living and connection to others.

References

Bacci, I. (2002). *The Art of Effortless Living.* TarcherPerigree.

Coulson, J. (2018). *10 Things Every Parent Needs to Know: Positive solutions for everyday parenting challenges.* ABC Books.

Tagore, R. (2004). *Stray Birds.* Cosimo Classics.

Thomas, A. (2019). *The Journal Writer's Companion.* Exisle Publishing.

Various other quotes retrieved 2019 from www.goodreads.com and https://quotefancy.com.

www.ingramcontent.com/pod-product-compliance
Lightning Source LLC
Chambersburg PA
CBHW041430010526
44107CB00046B/1563